D1549058

Class Cards

How to Put Your Class in the Palm of Your Hand

THIRD, EXPANDED EDITION

Rick Morris

Creator of New Management

Other Books by Rick Morris
Tools & Toys: Fifty Fun Ways to Love Your Class
The New Management Handbook:
A Step-By-Step Guide for Creating a Happier, More Productive Classroom

Teaching Guides by Rick Morris
Sentence Strips: Cut-and-Paste Paragraphs
The Home Education Bulletin

Class Cards
Copyright © 2001 by Rick Morris

New Management
6512 Edmonton Avenue
San Diego, California 92122

For information, you can call us at:
(858) 455-6000

or send e-mail to:
rick@teachers.net

or visit our website at:
http://www.newmanagement.com

I.S.B.N. 1-889236-08-X

Cover design
Len Torres

Cover art
Nate Robb

Illustrations
Alison & Peter Owen

Editor
Emily Morris

Not that we are sufficient of ourselves to think of anything
as being from ourselves, but our sufficiency comes from God.
—II Corinthians 3:5

for Gladys...
a mentor in the truest sense of the word

Table of Contents

Acknowledgements

As my friend and mentor, Len Torres, once told me:

No one creates in a vacuum.

With that in mind, let me start by saying thank you to Gladys Berner. A mentor teacher before we started officially recognizing and rewarding such special people, Gladys not only introduced me to the idea of CLASS CARDS but also inspired me with her personal pursuit of excellence in education.

Thanks to the following dedicated professionals at San Diego State University: Drs. Lloyd Kendall, Joe Duckworth, Bob McCabe, Anne Nagel, Lynn Fox, Sticks Rowland, Ray Ross, and Gerry Gates. Their encouragement and moral support have been (and will continue to be) truly inspirational and greatly appreciated.

Thanks to Dave Mittleholtz, former director of the Achievement Goals Program; Michael Forester and the folks at the Teaching and Learning Center; and Dr. Freda Callahan. My earliest days as a mentor with San Diego Unified School District wouldn't have been the same without their support.

Thanks to my teaching buddies: Mark Alcorn, Barbara Israel, JoAnn Stoll, and David Brown, friends and educators, for keeping a smile on my face.

Thanks to Dave Koeberle for believing in me.

Thanks to my sweet daughters, Emily and Alison, who helped me with this newest edition of my first book. Emily did a great job of editing the text while Alison and her husband, Peter, took care of the illustrations. I love you babies.

And to Len, whom I couldn't possibly thank enough.

About This Book

Class Cards is a teaching tool from the New Management system of student management, motivation, and involvement. This system is a refreshingly new and incredibly effective approach to the challenges educators face in today's classrooms. Initially developed in 1981, New Management has since undergone almost twenty years of classroom-tested refining and improvement. A simple yet efficient system, New Management is easy-to-learn and fun-to-use.

Since 1987, I have been sharing New Management's innovative teaching techniques with thousands of educators. The overwhelming consensus is:

New Management works.

From first year teachers to seasoned veterans, from the primary grades to the university level, New Management is enabling educators to teach more effectively and manage more efficiently. At the same time, it's empowering them to make fairness, firmness, and consistency an everyday reality.

New Management offers benefits for students, too. Teachers who use the New Management system provide their students with significant opportunities to become more responsible, productive, and involved. In fact, an increase in the level of student involvement and participation is one of the reasons teachers using New Management say their paperworking tasks go down while student motivation goes up. And when students and teachers are really working together, the potential for growth is without limits.

So, in an effort to reach even more educators, I decided to produce a series of teachers' guides. Because of its tremendous popularity, Class Cards was selected as the first technique from the New Management system to be offered in a written format. This teaching tool, like the New Management system itself, is simple and effective. Class Cards will not only raise your level of classroom control, but lower your level of stress: not a bad combination.

To begin with, picture yourself in class. You've just asked a question and you'd like one of your students to answer. Now then, which student should you call on to respond?

Should you call on one of the five or six eager hand wavers? How about asking that underachiever hiding out in the back of the room? Or maybe you should select one of the many students living in the Land of Semi-Involvement.

And while you're pondering this choice, don't forget about being fair. Are you giving everyone an equal chance to participate, or does the lion's share of these response opportunities go to just a chosen few?

Come along, now; make a decision. The class is beginning to get restless. What are you going to do? (Don't answer out loud. This is just a book. I can't hear you.)

Sound familiar? If you're like most of us, you find yourself engaged in this time-consuming, stress-inducing procedure a hundred times a day. Isn't there a better way?

Fortunately, there is.

Visualize a deck of playing cards. On the face of each card you have written the name of one of your students. (If, for instance, you have thirty students in your second grade class or thirty sophomores in your fifth period algebra class, you'd end up with thirty cards in your deck.) And now, to decide which student is going to respond to the question you've asked, just draw a card and call a name. It's that simple.

Using a deck of Class Cards to call on students during class discussions and learning activities will bring about a dramatic improvement in the quality of education in your room. You'll not only experience a positive change in your morale and performance, you'll witness a definite change in your students, as well.

Almost immediately you'll feel a major reduction in your level of stress. Among other things, this reduction in stress will translate into a sense of renewed energy. Released from the tedium of picking and choosing students to respond, you'll be free to concentrate on the direction, flow, and content of your lessons. As one grateful educator put it: "Class Cards was a much needed shot in a very tired arm."

Student motivation will be the next area to undergo a positive change. Due to the surprising randomness of the cards being drawn and the names being called, a deck of Class Cards will generate a wonderful air of anticipation. You'll soon find your students looking at class discussions in a new and exciting way. Teacher-student interactions will almost seem like a game show to them. With a nearly endless variety of "card tricks" available, you'll have the entire class in the palm of your hand, so to speak.

Finally, and perhaps most significantly, Class Cards will help you establish an equal opportunity learning environment. By promoting, and then maintaining, total class involvement, Class Cards will provide you with the power to maximize the growth and development of each and every student. From the overachievers to the underachievers, from the hand wavers to the seemingly handless, this dynamic teaching tool will boost your interactive effectiveness on a daily basis. With no conscious effort on your part, you'll have the ability to interact with your students in a manner which is fair, firm, and consistent: the hallmark of an effective educator.

This book was written to help you get started. By showing you how a set of Class Cards has met my needs, you'll discover how to meet your own. A technique which is completely open-ended, Class Cards is nearly boundless in its wide range of classroom applications. Within a few months, you'll be coming up with your own ideas for utilizing the power of this wonderfully simple tool. The more you use it, the better it will get. And the better it gets, the more you'll use it. Class Cards will become an indispensable aid for years to come.

Before too long you'll be asking yourself, "How did I ever teach without my cards?" Having used Class Cards for so many years now, I know I'd be lost without mine.

May they work as well for you and your students.

—Rick Morris
    December 20, 2000
    San Diego, California

Chapter 1

Getting Started

Making It Work

Card Tricks

Who dares to teach
must never cease to learn.

—John Cotton Dana

Chapter 1
Getting Started

Do you have what you need?

Apart from the desire to try new ideas with your students, the only things you are going to need in order to get started are:

✓ a deck of cards

✓ a permanent ink felt tip pen
  (a Sharpie® fine point works great)

✓ a class roster or seating chart

FIG. 1-1
It doesn't take much to make a set of Class Cards.

Making Your Set of Class Cards

Using a permanent ink, felt tip marker, write a student's name on the face of a playing card. [Fig. 1-2] You should probably write the name at both ends so that it will be readable no matter which end of the card turns up. Keep writing names until you have one card for each student.

FIG. 1-2
Here we see Tracy's card. Having the name on both ends of her card will make it easier to read and use.

FIG. 1-3
Keep writing names on cards until you have one card for each student.

When you've finished making your set of cards, put the pen you used and the extra cards in a place that is safe and out of the way. This will enable you to easily get your hands on them whenever you need to make a new card to add to your original set.

FIG. 1-4
Your card kit: the permanent ink felt tip pen and the extra cards in the original box.

A Word About Cards

Having used Class Cards for many years now, it's become apparent that some types of cards work better than others. The first set I saw was made from 3 X 5 index cards. Although they will work adequately, I've come to the conclusion that you just can't beat a good deck of jumbo-faced Bicycles®.

Using actual playing cards will provide you with several distinct advantages.

ADVANTAGE 1

Real playing cards are designed to be durable. One deck will easily endure a year's worth of use.

ADVANTAGE 1

ADVANTAGE 2

The jumbo-faced cards (marked Jumbo Index on the box) have an extra wide margin at the top and bottom for writing names.

ADVANTAGE 2

ADVANTAGE 3

A deck of real playing cards makes a great noise when you shuffle them. This distinctive sound will be an attention getter, to say the least.

ADVANTAGE 3

ADVANTAGE 4

After making your set of Class Cards, you'll have extra cards. These leftovers will be used later for newly enrolling students.

ADVANTAGE 4

In fact, the only imaginable drawback to using a deck of playing cards for making your set of Class Cards is the remote possibility that some people might be overly sensitive to the "gambling aspect" of these cards. Their focus would be upon the cards themselves and not the interactive tool inherent within.

Look at the four cards shown below, for example. Although you are clearly seeing *Ben, Emily, Alison,* and *Peter,* someone else might be focusing on the *7, 8, 9,* and *10 of spades.*

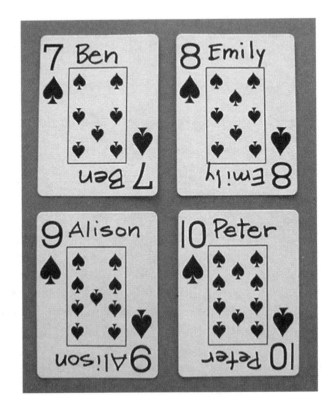

FIG. 1-5
Most people will see these cards as they are meant to be seen: a technique for treating all students fairly.

If this situation *were* to present itself, you could always spend a couple of bucks and order a set of blank-faced playing cards from one of the companies that produce them. Or maybe you could use a set of animal rummy cards or some such children's game set. Although this would require a bit of extra effort, it might just be worth your time. Class Cards is such a great idea that you won't want anything to slow you down nor will you want anyone to keep you from using it.

Reality: I've been using a set of Class Cards for over twenty years. Not once has anyone said anything that wasn't positive and supportive.

Adding New Cards to Your Deck

Filling out a card for a newly enrolling student is one of the first things we do as a class when someone officially checks in. It has proven to be such a great "ice breaker" that we've incorporated it into our welcoming routine for new students.

New Student Introduction Procedure

1. First, we stop all activities and turn our attention to our newest student.

2. While our new class member is introducing himself, I'll reach into my top desk drawer and grab the extra cards and pen.

3. I'll write the student's name on a new card.

4. After the card has been made, we'll make a ceremony of adding it to all of the others. (The class can always be counted on to provide a brief explanation about the significance of the cards.)

5. After assigning a partner to the student for the duration of the day, we'll resume our temporarily interrupted activities.

The bottom line is that new students are made to feel as if they are a part of the class from the minute they walk into the room. And the first time a new student's card comes up, he'll feel as if he's really "one of the gang."

So, keep the cards and pen in a special place. Having your card kit handy will reduce your level of stress, which will make it easier for you to smile at those new students as they enter your room.

Chapter 2

Getting Started

Making It Work

Card Tricks

*What we want to see is the child in pursuit of
knowledge, and not knowledge in pursuit of the child.*

— George Bernard Shaw

Chapter 2
Making It Work

Visualizing Success

The practice of seeing yourself do something before actually attempting to do it has been used with incredible success in business and professional sports. Since visualizing works in those areas, I felt it could work in the classroom as well. And so, for the past several years, I have been including visualization techniques in my daily teaching.

Here's a situation that could use a bit of visualization:

> *Imagine, if you will, that you are about to ask your students to work outside on the grass near your classroom. They'll be working in cooperative learning groups on a social studies activity. In your mind, you can clearly see what it is you expect them to do. All you have to do is verbally direct them to that end.*

TEACHER
  Addressing students:
  I'd like you all to go outside and sit on the grass with your team. We're going to do a special social studies activity.

At first glance, this request appears to be reasonable and clearly stated. Unfortunately, though, it will most likely produce chaos and confusion. The chaos will be the result of the "Play Premise" at work. As we know, students operate on the principle that just about anything can be turned into an opportunity for fun and games. The confusion will stem from a lack of clarity because the stated request does little to create a workable mental image of the action to be performed. In fact, of all the words spoken in the teacher's directions to the students, the only things the students actually heard and visualized were:

Blah blah blah blahhhh de blah **outside** *de blah blahh* **grass** *blah de blahde blah. Blah blah-blah de blah-de-blah blah blahlala.*

Too often with students, our words—as they hear them—don't always mean what we intend them to mean.

A STUDENT'S GLOSSARY OF TEACHER TERMINOLOGY

Teacher says:	Student interprets:
outside	Loud, unstructured fun!
grass	Let's wrestle and push!

Thus, you shouldn't be too surprised to find your students cavorting about with gleeful abandon when you finally join them outside. They're merely being kids.

Let's experiment with some visualization and see if we might be able to create in their minds an actual image of what we want them to do.

MR. MORRIS
Speaking to his students:

Close your eyes for a moment. Listen to my words as they describe something we are all going to do. Imagine that everyone in class is getting up and calmly sliding chairs under the desks. Students are then walking outside to the grassy area. When they get outside, they find their teammates and sit together on the grass. You can probably picture yourself sitting with your own team. As you look around, you can see the other teams sitting together—almost like little islands in a green sea. And now, here comes Mr. Morris with a special social studies activity.

(Slight pause for the image to set.)

That's what I'd like you to do now. Open your eyes and let's make it happen.

Think of how much more successful these students will be merely because I took thirty seconds to paint a clear picture of what they are supposed to do. Visualization works.

Continue to visualize success by picturing yourself in front of your class. You have your set of Class Cards in your hand. Additionally, you have everyone's undivided attention. You're feeling relaxed, productive, and in control. Your students are thinking and responding to your lesson. Everyone—from high achiever to low—is right with you: thinking, learning, growing. That's quite a picture!

With the Class Cards in your hand, you won't believe how easily a lesson can flow because now you'll know exactly who to call upon for a response. With all of the decisions we have to make each and every day, this decision-free tool will be a real stress reducer.

FIG. 2-1
Visualize being relaxed, productive, and in control.

And regardless of how individual students actually respond when called on, using your Class Cards on a regular basis will ensure, *with no conscious effort on your part*, that everyone in your class is being given an equal opportunity to participate in the learning process.

Sound like fun? You bet it is! Granted, it's going to take a bit of time for your students to adjust to the demands these cards will place upon their level of classroom awareness. It's a learned behavior, and you'll be learning right along with them. Within a month or two, you and your class will be well on your way to attaining a true equal opportunity learning environment.

Note: Don't skim over the words "a month or two" in the preceding sentence too quickly. We're talking four to eight weeks before this technique really begins to work well. That's a lot of time. Nonetheless, education is a process, and it's important to keep long-range goals in mind. By introducing teaching practices slowly, and then allowing sufficient time for these techniques to become comfortable and natural extensions of your daily interactions, you'll be setting the stage for a successful year. Six weeks may seem like a long time; but, it pales in comparison to the amount of time you'll be spending with your students from the first day in September through the last day of school in June.

So, be patient, take your time, and focus on the positive. Think about how great it will be when you and your Class Cards are really "cookin'."

Visualizing success is just one of the steps toward overall success. As I tell my students: "See it happen, make it happen." If you *see* yourself using Class Cards successfully, you'll be helping to *make* Class Cards work successfully.

FIG. 2-2
This sign, which hangs in our classroom, helps to remind students about the power of visualizing.

See it happen, make it happen.

Introducing Class Cards to Your Students

So far, a quick review shows that you've got your cards in your hand and you've already done some visualizing. At this point, you're saying to yourself, "Now what?"

First of all, pick an appropriate time to introduce Class Cards to your students. Make your description of this tool—and the reasons behind its use—both positive and supportive. Students might be inclined to suspect the worst, being the skeptical little people they sometimes are. Reassure them that Class Cards is a fair and fun technique for realizing everyone's highest potential.

Make sure that your students see these cards as they are meant to be seen: an incredibly powerful tool for maximizing the growth and development of *all* students.

The following list contains a few of the points I emphasize when I introduce Class Cards to each new class.

1

Class Cards are fair.
Everyone gets a chance to participate. No one will have that "left out" feeling.

2

Class Cards help students become more responsible.
Everyone will learn to pay attention to what is going on in class since we won't know whose card is coming up.

3

Class Cards are fun.
The suspense and drama of the games you can play will lend a wonderful air of anticipation and excitement to your discussions and lessons, leaving them begging for more. (*Caution*: They might not believe you on this point just yet. It will take a few fun interactions with the cards before they'll be truly convinced. See Chapter Three: *Card Tricks* for some suggestions about having a good time with your cards.)

4

Class Cards help students become better responders.
The added wait time you can incorporate into your question-and-answer sessions will have a dramatic impact upon the quality of responses they will begin to generate.

Regardless of what you *say* by way of an introduction to the Class Cards technique, the awareness your students will develop is going to require actual *use* of your Class Cards. A brief introduction, though, will certainly help to ensure that no one is taken by surprise.

Stating Your Expectations

Your students have now been introduced to your Class Cards, and you have provided them with many reasons for their use. They've actually seen the cards with their names on them. The time has now come to explain very clearly the students' roles and to answer some important questions.

What part do the students play?

What are their obligations?

What is it you expect of them?

Let your students know that they will be expected to develop answers to your questions as you present them. State your expectations clearly and concisely. Make them a class pledge.

You could even make a sign that reflects your basic expectations.

I figure out the answers to questions when they are asked.

FIG. 2-3
Here's another classroom sign. This one gently reminds students to be ready to respond.

Nonetheless, you shouldn't expect your students to suddenly sit up and get involved in discussions and lessons merely because you happen to have a deck of cards in your hand. For many students, this new interactive technique of yours will be a major departure from what has been a very comfortable life of non-involvement.

I believe that poor mental attitudes in students are partially due to the years of conditioning they've received at the hands of their teachers. As long as there have been teachers and students, the game has been: "Raise your hand if you wish to participate and respond." Conversely, students who keep their hands down expect to be left out of the lesson. Since they are not expecting to be called upon, they do not prepare a response other than the time-honored: "Why did you call on me? I didn't have my hand up."

Now that you won't always be calling on students according to who has a hand up, you'll want to encourage them to develop the art of being prepared to respond to all of your questions and comments.

The attitude of readiness that you will want to nurture can be communicated to your class in many different ways.

Here are four possibilities:

TEACHER
Addressing students:

Begin figuring out the answer to my question as soon as I present it.

Please don't wait until I call your name to start thinking.

Come up with an answer every time you hear a question.

Be prepared to respond before you hear your name called.

Actually, the phrase I use most often is:

"Have an answer ready, please."

Realistically speaking, the attainment of this "be prepared" attitude is going to be an on-going—yet worthy—project. Eventually, though, with the repetitive practice that Class Cards will provide for your class *and* the positive reinforcement you'll give them for their efforts, your students will begin to sit up and get involved in lessons merely because you have a deck of cards in your hand. Just be sure to state your expectations clearly and then "be prepared" to help everyone live up to them.

Response Awareness

For the record, response opportunities come in many forms encompassing everything from "taking a turn at oral reading" to "sharing feelings"; from "choosing sides for a game" to "point to where we are in the book." The spectrum runs from make-believe to self-evaluation and back again.

So, whenever you see me refer to student responses, please don't limit your awareness to situations in which a student is answering a direct question. That might be the case some of the time; however, there's a whole world of response opportunities just waiting to be used.

Time Out!

Even with the most thorough introduction of Class Cards and numerous attempts at communicating the fine art of response readiness, randomly selecting students to respond might still find them unprepared at first.

If—when calling someone's name—you can see that the student doesn't have an answer ready or is now scrambling to find out where you are in the book, take a moment to deal with the situation. Although we want to emphasize the positive, don't be afraid to call "Time Out!" when you see that a student needs a verbal reminder about your expectations regarding involvement and preparedness.

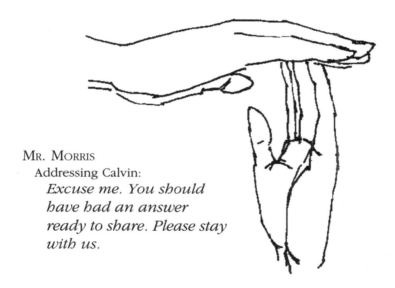

MR. MORRIS
  Addressing Calvin:
    *Excuse me. You should
    have had an answer
    ready to share. Please stay
    with us.*

After making these comments, I'll usually set aside Calvin's card as a reminder to check on him in a few minutes. When called upon the second time, he should be able to demonstrate that he's now "keeping up with" the lesson.

I find that I have to do this kind of gentle reinforcing for the first few weeks of card use. It's just another way of letting them know how serious I am about my expectations regarding awareness, responsibility, and self-discipline.

Note: From my experience, I've found that for every corrective "Time Out!" there have been ten "thank you's," three "well said's," and a dozen non-verbal signs recognizing students who *were* ready to respond.

Win-Win (You-Students)

And now, here's a brief word about the power of your Class Cards. With the cards in hand, you'll be placing yourself in a position of increased power as a teacher. This will be an enhancement of your existing power as primary educator and adult figure. It's a power we sometimes underestimate.

By using Class Cards, you'll not only have every student within your grasp, you'll also have the ability to "spotlight" any one of them. And let's face it, some of them have not been the focus of this "spotlight" for some time now.

I'm referring to the underachievers, the disruptors, the shy and soft-spoken—the ones who have trained their teachers, through a variety of manipulative techniques, that it is not rewarding to call upon them. Go easy on these students at first. Although you don't want to compromise your educational principles nor undermine your expectations of student preparedness, you *do* want to be careful to *not* abuse your authority.

You'll want to make sure that you're using the cards for "calling on" students as opposed to "picking on" students.

You'll want to ensure that you're not using the cards to find out which students aren't prepared, but to encourage them all to be ready to respond: not to find out who isn't paying attention, but to nurture and develop attentiveness by instilling the self-discipline necessary for such a skill.

Use your cards as the teaching-learning device they were meant to be and not the disciplinary weapon they could all too easily become.

With your Class Cards in hand, you'll be in control. It's guaranteed. You'll have the freedom to call on your students without the interference of stress-inducing decision making. You'll have a teaching technique which not only promotes student self-awareness and self-discipline but continues to reinforce it as well.

You'll have the entire class in the palm of your hand.

At this point in time, *you* are already winning. Now, it's up to you to make sure that *your students* become winners. Win-Win means *everyone* is feeling successful with your Class Cards: you *and* your students.

By focusing on the second Win (Students), you'll be adding immeasurably to the first Win (You).

See it happen, make it happen.

"I Don't Know Yet."

One sure-fire way to promote student success with your Class Cards is to allow them the opportunity to tell you that they don't know the answer to a question. This is especially important for your underachievers. Having a "way out" when called upon helps to increase student involvement. It will also help to produce a low affective filter: that is, a learning environment of reduced anxiety.

Although it's good to have high goals and expectations for your students, it's equally important to remain realistic about their range of abilities. How adept are they at processing information, developing appropriate responses, and stating answers[†] in front of the class? Be realistic in your expectations. Remember that even adults have fears, some of which are depicted in the following chart:

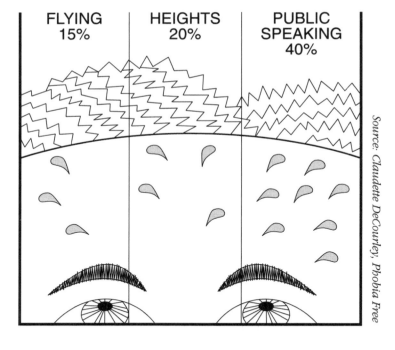

FIG. 2-4
Three common adult fears and the percentage of adults who suffer from these fears.

Note: Each drop of perspiration represents 7 million people.

FLYING 15%   HEIGHTS 20%   PUBLIC SPEAKING 40%

Source: Claudette DeCourley, Phobia Free

Some students are going to need more time to come up with a successful response, whereas others are going to require some prompting. Since we're being completely realistic about the matter, we might as well accept this fact: some students are just going to need actual practice with the art of response in order to become successful, confident responders.

---

† Here's something to keep in mind: Just because a responding student isn't standing in front of the class doesn't mean he isn't speaking before a group of people. The fear of speaking in front of a large group of people is very common in adults, let alone children. Do you ever wonder how all of those adults got to be so phobic in the first place?

So, allow them the opportunity to say that they don't know what's going on, if that happens to be the case. At least you've been given a response. And if you're going to allow them to respond in this way (a definite Win-Win), you might as well maximize the opportunity.

Instruct your students who don't know an answer to respond with the phrase:

"I don't know yet."

This simple statement is much more powerful than the standard "I don't know" reflex response.

By adding the word *yet*, the student is subconsciously affirming that he plans to know the answer shortly. *He is going to figure out what the answer is at some point in the lesson.* The word "yet" gives learning a more immediate sense. The idea that learning and understanding occur on a continuing basis sends a strong message to all of your students, not just the one responding.

Suggestion: When a student responds with "I don't know yet," you might want to set his card aside. This will remind you to call on him later in the lesson. Before calling on this student again, try to make sure that he has had a chance to learn and understand what it was he didn't know in the first place. With a bit of practice (and patience), you can turn every "I don't know yet" situation into a positive learning opportunity.

FIG. 2-5
A card set aside as a reminder to get back to this student (Alberto) after a couple of other students have been called upon.

In a nutshell: "I don't know" is the past. "I don't know yet" is the future.

Encouraging Student Support

In the first edition of Class Cards, I made the following statement:

> *"Student support of your Class Cards, although not absolutely necessary in order for them to be used with success, will really boost their value."*

I take it back. I was wrong. You'll want your students to enjoy this technique.

Student support will not only increase your desire to use your Class Cards but will add immeasurably to their overall effectiveness. Fortunately, there are many methods for developing and maintaining student interest, support, and acceptance.

The use of positive reinforcement seems to be an obvious first choice.

Even though we are already doing this to a great extent when we embrace a Win-Win philosophy, I want to make sure that we all keep in mind how powerful a positive mindset can be. For some students, being treated in a positive manner makes all the difference in the world.

Be patient with students who continue to raise hands when you're trying to use your cards.

At first, it took a bit of time for some of my students to break their automatic habit of raising a hand in response to my questions. To help recondition them, I simply held up the cards and said, "He's got the cards." Within a week or two, I had students who were softly saying it for me as I showed the deck in my hand to the few die-hard hand wavers.

FIG. 2-6

Just show them the deck you're using as a signal to lower their hands.

Don't always use the cards during your interactions.

Give them a rest every now and then by allowing students to raise their hands to volunteer responses. This will become especially important as your students become more successful responders and, thus, begin to develop a desire to share their thoughts more often.

This duality of interaction via cards versus raised hands could pose a challenge for your students, though. When do I raise my hand? When should I wait to be called upon? How will I know what is appropriate?

In an effort to address these student concerns and avoid any undo confusion, I've taken to using American Sign Language. Sign language is simple to use and easy to understand.

When I'd like students to raise a hand to be called on for a voluntary response, I'll raise my own hand and form the letter "v." (I usually put down the deck of cards or hide it behind my back). This sign gives the green light to hand raising.

FIG. 2-7
This sign means that I'd like somone to raise a hand and volunteer an answer.

Sometimes, during discussions or lessons, I'd like a group response. The sign for a spontaneous oral answer is the same "v" for volunteer, but I'll hold the sign next to my ear. This lets them know it's okay to "blurt out" an answer.

FIG. 2-8
This sign means that it's okay to say your answer out loud.

General rule: Blurting out an answer when I haven't asked for one is not okay. See Red Hands, page 48, for a simple way to deal with this situation.

Encourage positive listening from your students.

Students need to understand that not all wisdom and knowledge come from just the teacher. Other students can often be fountains of knowledge during discussions. Unfortunately, they usually don't pay attention to one another. They're either focused on you, themselves, or nothing at all. So, to help reinforce the fine art of positive listening, I'll call on someone to repeat a response just given by a student.

> *Important Factor:*
> It should be explained here that I don't engage in "echoing." That is, I do not repeat student responses so that everyone can hear what one student has just said. I understand the motivation behind this practice: some students don't speak loudly enough for everyone to hear and, as concerned teachers, we are merely repeating pertinent information.
>
> Good intentions notwithstanding, echoing can be damaging in the long run. I do enough speaking as it is without being Mr. Microphone for half my class. Another down-side is that the students who are not speaking with enough volume will never develop this important skill if they know the teacher will rebroadcast their statements for them.
>
> One last thought has to do with respect. If a student shares information or thoughts or critical thinking that is worthy of echoing, the student himself should be the one to restate it. Otherwise, I'll just end up reinforcing the perception that the important stuff will come from my mouth, which, in its own circular way, produces poor listening skills.
>
> So, back off just a bit. If some of your students are not speaking so that others can clearly hear what is being said, let them deal with it.
>
> *P.S.* If you're still not convinced that you should give up the time-honored technique of echoing student responses, check out the article on my website entitled, "Confessions of a Former Echoer." [The New Management URL is http://www.newmanagement.com]

Years ago, when I began to call upon students to repeat the answer that another student had just given, a lot of them responded with, "I didn't hear what he said." In fact, I heard this stock response so often that I decided to do something about it.

Here's what I came up with:

FIG. 2-9
Students say "Echo" whenever they didn't hear what was just said in class by another student.

It's a simple procedure that reinforces the concept of students being responsible for their own education. (It is also beneficial for the soft-spoken members of your class who need to improve their speaking skills.) Now that students will no longer be able to sing that same old tune of "I didn't hear what he said," they will eventually become more attentive and active listeners.

Reality: If I were a student in class, and I didn't clearly hear what Calvin has just said, I would raise my hand and say, "Echo" because I never know when Mr. Morris is going to ask me to repeat Calvin's gem of wisdom.

Repetitive responses can be a real boon to the underachievers in your room.

As educators, we generally stop taking responses to a question as soon as we hear or see the correct answer. It's another one of those time-honored teaching traditions that needs to be reexamined. Here's an example from a social studies lesson that shows how it normally goes:

MR. MORRIS
Can someone tell me what city is the capital of California? Charmaine?

> CHARMAINE
> *Los Angeles?*
>
> MR. MORRIS
> *No, not Los Angeles. Dino?*
>
> DINO
> *San Francisco?*
>
> MR. MORRIS
> *Nooooo. Luke?*
>
> LUKE
> *Sacramento?*
>
> MR. MORRIS
> *Right you are! Now then, what goes on in the state capital? Why is it important? Alex?*

The correct answer sometimes flies right past many of our students. They didn't really have the chance to focus on it and see it clearly in their own minds.

I'm not sure why we typically move on to the next point of discussion once a question has been answered. It could be due to the training we received as students. Since our own teachers interacted with *us* in this manner, maybe we've been conditioned to perpetuate this practice. Or, maybe it's a matter of expediency. Who knows?

Repetitive responses that allow more than one student to provide a correct response to the same question will provide added impact to the actual answer and, ultimately, the learning process.

Here's an example of the way I do it now:

> MR. MORRIS
> *What is the capital of California?*
> (Drawing a card.)
> *Charmaine?*
>
> CHARMAINE
> *Los Angeles?*
>
> MR. MORRIS
> *Thank you.*

(Drawing another card.)
Luke?

LUKE
Sacramento?

MR. MORRIS
Thanks, Luke.
(Another card is drawn.)
Alex, what do you think?

ALEX
I think it's Sacramento.

ANOTHER STUDENT (WHO DIDN'T HEAR ALEX'S RESPONSE)
Echo.

ALEX (A LITTLE LOUDER THAN BEFORE)
I think it's Sacramento.

MR. MORRIS
I appreciate it when you guys ask
each other to repeat answers you didn't hear.
(Drawing another card.)
Jason? The capital of California?

JASON (AFTER A LENGTHY PAUSE)
I don't know yet.

MR. MORRIS
All right.
(Setting Jason's card aside and drawing another one.)
Lourena? What do you think?

LOURENA
Los Angeles.

MR. MORRIS
Thank you, Lourena.
(Drawing the next card.)
Sarah?

SARAH
Sacramento.

MR. MORRIS
    Many of you knew that Sacramento is our state capital. Now then, what goes on in the state capital? Why is it so important?
(Picking up Jason's card again.)
    Jason, what was the name of our state capital?

JASON
    Sacramento.

MR. MORRIS
    Thanks. So, what kinds of things happen in Sacramento?

There are three distinct advantages to calling upon many students for the same response even though the correct answer has already been given.

The first advantage is that you take your focus off of who is responding and place it on the concept being developed. Instead of praising the first student to supply the correct response, you allow multiple correct responses and enable many students to share and reinforce their knowledge.

The second advantage stems from the fact that you're not validating answers as you hear them. (My own responses are rather simple. "Thank you," "Uh-huh," or a nod of my head is all they need.) Then, after receiving many responses—some right, some wrong—you can let them know what the correct response was. This simple shift leads to the third advantage: a low affective filter[†].

By calling on several students for the answer to one question and reserving the validation for the end, you'll foster a setting in which it becomes safer for students to share their thoughts.

The "old school" standard had the teacher move on to the next question after hearing the correct response. By doing this, though, you are basically creating an environment in which you validate answers as being right or wrong. Right answer…you ask the next question. Wrong answer…you ask another student. Sounds innocuous, but certain students—insecure, timid, or underachieving—might refrain from giving an answer for fear of being wrong. How will everyone know it's wrong? The teacher will ask another student for a response.

Try letting many students supply the correct response and see what happens. I think you'll like the results.

Call on everyone.
Depending upon the importance of what is being covered in the lesson, I

---

†   Remember: decreased anxiety = increased learning.

sometimes want each student to respond. It only takes a minute or two and is a quick way of assessing the exact extent of student knowledge.

First, I'll ask the question. Then, I'll start going through the deck. As the students respond, I'll put the cards in piles according to their answer. After the last student has had a chance to respond, I'll pick up the stack of cards representing the correct response and verbally reinforce the answer.

FIG. 2-10
It's fun to go through the entire deck and allow each student to answer the same question.

Suggestion: Total class responses work especially well with either/or, true/false, or multiple choice questions.

Find ways to increase the wait time between the question you ask and the answers being given.

According to the research, ("Wait Time: Slowing Down May Be a Way of Speeding Up!") additional wait time will be beneficial to *all* of your students, not just the underachievers. With increased wait time, you'll experience increases in the length of student responses, a heightened sense of confidence in the responses being offered, and more student-to-student interaction.

So, don't feel you need to rush through your question/answer sessions. Allow them time to think and ponder. Nonetheless, see if you can develop a few techniques for increasing the wait time while also meeting the needs of your students who process information more quickly.

For example, one way to give underachievers more time to formulate an answer is to take silent responses from those students who appear to be ready. I'll say, "Silent answers, please." Students who wish to respond will raise a "v" hand. As I point at students, they mouth the answer which I can lip read. A nod, a wink, or a smile will let them know that their response was correct. After taking a number of these silent answers, I'll then use my Class Cards and call on students for oral responses.

Aside from the entertainment value of watching my students try to mouth the words, taking silent answers has proven to be a very effective method for maintaining total class involvement while providing more time for students to develop a response.

Use the cards of absent students in a positive way.
There will be times when you'll draw the card of someone who is absent. Do you skip over that name or set the card aside for the remainder of the day?

Skipping over the card might be misconstrued by the students as an act of unfairness on your part. Although you'll be clear as to why you are moving Jerome's card to the bottom of the deck—he's absent—some of your students might think that the card you just passed over was theirs. (The key words are *fair*, firm, consistent.)

The drawback to setting aside the card of an absent student is that you might not return the card to the deck at the end of the day. (Experience has shown me that children are extremely sensitive about being excluded from the set of Class Cards. In fact, a friend of mine told me about one of her underachievers who, when speaking to her privately, began to cry about the fact that his card wasn't in the deck with the others. Sure enough, when she checked, the card was missing. (Maybe you should do a brief roll call once a month to check the contents of your deck.)

Anyway, let's get back to the absent student, Jerome, and the fact that his card has been drawn. How about this idea: The first student to raise his hand and ask, "May I take Jerome's place?" will be allowed to respond. This playful variation will not only give everyone an extra chance at participating, but will prevent the card of the absent student from becoming a nuisance.

Try to keep it fun whenever possible.
Having a good time with the cards (yet another form of positive reinforcement) goes a long way in earning student support, participation, and attention. According to Bill Glasser, author of "The Quality School Teacher," there are five basic student needs that must be met on a regular basis in order for your students to become involved in the learning process. Fun is one of them. You'll find ideas in the next chapter, *Card Tricks*, that deal specifically with promoting the fun side of your Class Cards.

These simple strategies, *plus the ones you'll soon be coming up with on your own*, will lend credence to your initial claims that your set of Class Cards is going to enable students to grow and develop educationally in a new and exciting way. By keeping your interactions fresh and upbeat, you'll be encouraging your students to stay active and involved. After all, learning requires enthusiasm.

What Can You Expect?

From the very start, you can expect great things. Almost immediately, you'll feel a reduction in your level of stress. This is due to the fact that stress is caused by a feeling of not being in control of a situation. With your Class Cards in hand, you'll begin to experience a degree of classroom control you might not have thought possible. Both of these factors—the increase in control and the resulting decrease in your level of stress—will have a significant impact on your effectiveness as an educator.

At the same time, you'll see a wonderful student transformation. With just a bit of practice and experience, they will develop the habit of paying attention and being prepared which will dramatically enhance their overall motivation and involvement. As you already know, students who are motivated and involved are students who are learning, growing, and developing.

That's a lot to expect from a deck of cards. Nonetheless, twenty years of Class Cards experience has convinced me that you can look forward to even more benefits. After three to four months of regular card use, you'll begin to observe two rather subtle changes in your students.

Developmental Corollary #1

Due to the students' heightened awareness of the possibility of being called on to respond at any moment, more and more of them will develop the ability to know when they don't have enough information to provide a correct response. They become sensitive to, and concerned about, situations in which they are just not understanding whatever concept is being taught or discussed. Along with this awareness comes an incentive to seek help before the lesson progresses any further (or their cards are drawn!).

Consequently, you'll see more and more of your students asking for either further explanations of the concept or additional examples to illustrate its application. No longer will they wait until *you* find out they aren't mastering certain skills. They will do it for you. Your students will actually become self-diagnosing: a skill that will contribute to the success of your lessons and the ultimate, overall academic progress of your class.

Helpful: Students are more inclined to ask for clarification if they have a safe, predictable way in which to ask. The one line we've all heard when someone is confused during a lesson is: "I don't get it!" I sometimes feel this statement is made more from a sense of frustration than a quest for knowledge.

I finally taught my students how to ask for help when they found themselves stuck. A simple, "Could you do a sample?" usually clears up most of the ambiguity. It basically tells me to stop talking and start showing. This phrase is safe. It doesn't mean that the student is hopelessly lost or not teachable. It just means that he or she would like to see a different version of what you are trying to explain.

Developmental Corollary #2

As a result of the high frequency of random opportunities Class Cards will provide your students for responding in class, responding will soon become an acquired skill. All of this repetitive practice, in conjunction with your continuous support, will ultimately increase their confidence at responding.

In no time at all you'll begin to see more and more students volunteering to respond. Many of these volunteers will be students you never would have thought would volunteer for anything. You weren't even sure they possessed a hand to raise let alone the confidence and desire to raise it. But there they'll be, ready to jump in and get involved…wanting to get a firm grip on their own education…wanting to be the very best students they can possibly be.

And all of this for $2.49: the price of a deck of cards? It's hard to believe that so much could be had for so little.

Chapter 3

Getting Started

Making It Work

Card Tricks

Learning requires enthusiasm.

—Rick Morris

Card Tricks

A Spoonful of Honey

I can practically guarantee that Class Cards will significantly improve your interactive effectiveness when used in the basic draw-a-card-and-call-a-name mode. Nonetheless, the spice that a variety of card techniques can add to the life of your daily educational program should not be overlooked. A "spoonful of honey," as they say, "makes the medicine go down". Not that education should be likened unto castor oil, mind you. It's just that, in the motivational scheme of things, having a good time is hard to beat.

Group Activities

Anytime you need to informally group your students for an activity, you could use your Class Cards.

> *Need five groups? Shuffle the cards and deal out five "hands." Pick up the first pile of cards and call out the names. Hand these cards to one of the students from that group. This student can then make sure everyone whose name was just called gathers together.*

This quick and easy technique will get the students more involved and active while making group management and organization easier for you.

Now that they are in their groups, how about letting the students use the cards as they interact with each other?

> *Does the group need to assign some student tasks? Do they want to be fair about taking turns and ensure that everyone has a chance to participate? They could use the cards to help instill a sense of fairness and equity.*

Shuffle the cards and then place them face down in the middle of the group.

Turn the top card and have that student perform, or take care of, one of the group tasks. Keep drawing cards from the pile until everyone has been given a chance to participate in some fashion.

> *Want to work on communication skills? Want to promote positive listening and ensure that only one person is speaking at one time? Use the cards.*

Everyone in the group holds his/her own personal card. A student "takes the floor" by putting his card face up in the middle of the group. He's now free to speak until he picks up his card. The next student who wishes to speak drops his card in the middle of the group and has his say.

Suggestion: Allow your students the opportunity to work out the finer points of group card use. For instance, let them decide what to do when two cards are dropped in the middle of the group at the same time. What does the group do if someone wants to talk on and on? Etc., etc.

Center Stage

There occur times when I need to have every student speak in front of the class. Oral reading of a creative writing assignment provides a good example. To make sure that everyone gets a chance to speak and no one is overlooked, I use my Class Cards.

I'll shuffle the cards and deal out three cards face up in front of me. The three names on these cards are announced. (The remaining cards are set aside in a pile.)

FIG. 3-1
After hearing their names called, Dang, Van, and Crystal head to the front of the classroom to make their oral presentations.

The first student called knows he's first and heads to the front of the room to read.

Students Two and Three know they are next and take a moment to prepare themselves.

After Student One is finished reading, I collect his assignment and turn my attention to Student Two, who should be making his way to the front of the room. Two reads and then hands in his assignment. Finally, Three reads and his assignment is collected.

When all three have finished, three new cards are drawn and placed on top of the first three. We won't stop until all cards have been drawn.

This strategy ensures that you will hear from everyone. It's a fool-proof method which will prevent you from overlooking anyone who might be trying to "hide out" because he hasn't finished the assignment. When you play Center Stage, anyone not finished would know to stand and say "I'm not finished yet" when called upon to read.

"Beat the Book"

In a *typical* lesson, we usually proceed to the written product to show individual mastery of subject material after the actual teaching/learning portion of the lesson has been concluded. There are times, though, when I'd rather try to end the lesson on a more positive note. I'm talking about the kind of lessons where the answers are relatively obvious, and the written product is not essential to learning[†].

By playing a round of "Beat the Book," you'll not only eliminate the "busy work" aspect of some assignments, you'll also nurture the team work concept while improving the students' ability to concentrate.

Here is a scenario that illustrates the basic idea behind "Beat the Book":

MR. MORRIS
Addressing students at the conclusion of a simple lesson:
*Well, it says in my teacher's guide that you are now supposed to figure out whether these ten sentences are telling sentences or question sentences. The directions say to write a **T for telling** or a **Q for question.***

---

† "The important stuff goes on up here," I tell my students, as I point to my head. "Pushing a pencil isn't always learning."

Let's try something different. How about Beat the Book?
(Shuffling the cards.)
Let's see. Ten sentences? All right, let's find ten contestants.
(Dealing out ten cards face down on the desk.)
One, two, three, four, five, six, seven, eight, nine, ten! If these ten students can give us ten correct responses, then you will have shown me that you understand this lesson and we can move on to other things.
(Setting remainder of deck aside.)
Any last questions before I call the first contestant? Okay…Sentence #1. Is it a telling sentence or a question sentence? Please don't guess. We're all counting on you. Maybe you should check the punctuation mark.
(Turning over the first card.)
Marshall? Answer please?

MARSHALL
Telling.

MR. MORRIS
You've got it! Tell us how you knew it was a telling sentence.

MARSHALL
Because I can see a period at the end of the sentence.

MR. MORRIS
Way to go, Marshall. One down, nine to go. Sentence #2. Telling or question? Concentrate on this one.
(Students are now starting to look up and smile as they find the answer.)
I can tell some of you already know the answer. Here we go.
(Turning over the next card.)
Angela?

ANGELA
It's a telling sentence.

MR. MORRIS
Correct!
(Mild student huzzahs can be heard.)
On to sentence 3. Is it a telling sentence or a question sentence?

Etc., etc.

If, when called upon, a student cannot answer correctly or does not know which sentence we're talking about or engages in any of a number of incorrect response modes, the game is over. The "book beat them," and they must, therefore, complete the actual written assignment as detailed in the teacher's guide.

Since I know that the class won't be terribly thrilled with Calvin if he were to answer incorrectly, I always make a point of defusing what could become an unpleasant situation.

MR. MORRIS

Now then, do you think he was trying to make a mistake? I don't think so. Would you try to mess up on purpose? No way! Hey, he did his best. So let's go ahead and do the written part. Remember, that's what you were supposed to have done anyway.

Challenge: See if you can turn a "lost game" into an opportunity for reteaching. Discuss why the incorrect response was given, and use it to your advantage the next time you play.

The following example shows a situation in which we learned—and profited from!—one of our past mistakes.

MR. MORRIS

Addressing the students at the end of another lesson:
Okay, let's play "Beat the Book" with this assignment. Before we begin, though, can anyone tell us why we lost the last game?

STUDENT

Yeah, someone gave us the answer to a sentence we weren't doing yet.

MR. MORRIS

Well then, you might want to keep your finger right on the sentence we're doing. That way you won't get lost and give an incorrect answer. Ready? Here we go!

There will be many times, though, when your class actually "beats the book." This means that all of the questions were answered correctly. Even the under-achievers contributed a few correct responses. Wow, what a morale booster for your students! They'll be "on top of the world".

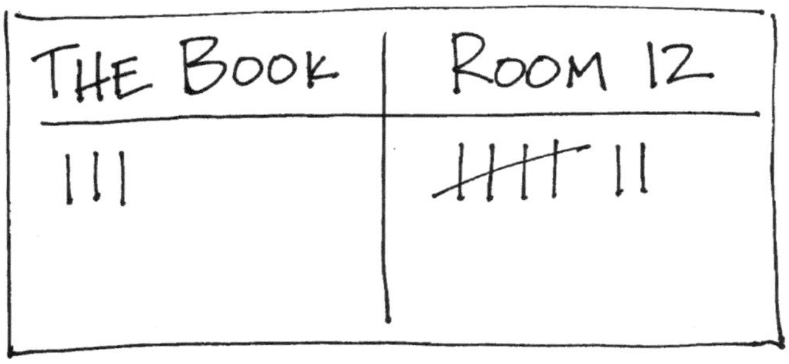

FIG. 3-2
You might want to keep a simple scoreboard in your room showing the current score.

THE BOOK	ROOM 12

First Name Bingo

Here's a simple little game, courtesy of Barbara Israel, ace teacher and good friend, that you can play with your students at the beginning of the year to acquaint them with their classmates and to also let them see the fun side of Class Cards.

1. Start by asking everyone to make a game card. [Fig. 3-3]
2. Have them walk about the room with card and pencil in hand and collect first names from one another.
3. Once cards have been filled, decide what type of bingo will be played. [*Four Corner; Diagonal; Longitude;* and *Latitude* are shown in Fig. 3-4.]
4. Shuffle your Class Cards and start reading names.
5. As students hear names, they mark out the matching ones.
6. Without too much prompting, someone will soon scream out "BINGO!"

FIRST NAME BINGO

Jason	Travis	Alex	Quang	~~Andre~~
Dylan	~~Mary~~	~~Ki~~	Dion	Jesus
~~Jenny~~	Kyle	~~FREE~~	Maria	Calvin
Dani	Jean	Brian	~~Tracy~~	Dang
~~Ben~~	Sheri	Mike	Ty	Sarah

FIG. 3-3
This bingo card holds 24 names.

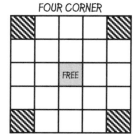
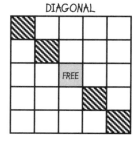
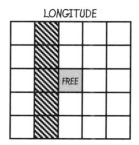
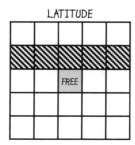

FIG. 3-4
These are the four basic games we play.

Speed Math

This game is a quick and playful way to see how well my students are understanding math concepts. We usually play whenever I'm giving them an activity sheet which culminates a week's worth of lessons. By playing Speed Math before allowing them their thirty minutes of independent work time, I'll get a feel for who needs a bit of private reteaching.

To play this game you'll need 8 1/2 X 11 newsprint, an activity sheet or assignment of some type, and your set of Class Cards.

1. Prepare newsprint answer sheets by folding them twice. [Fig. 3-5.] Keep folded during play.
2. Pass out activity sheets.
3. Determine how long your students will need to complete one problem.
4. Announce the time limit (60 seconds) and the problem they are to solve. (Don't start with #1; mix it up a bit.)
5. Tell them to begin (work is done in one of the answer sheet spaces) and then stop them when the time is up.
6. Using your cards, call out the names of five students. These students will then come see you with their answer sheets. Set aside the cards of anyone who is showing you an incomplete or incorrect answer. Call a few more names and take oral responses. Set aside more cards if necessary.
7. Announce the correct answer.
8. Keep playing until you've done four or five problems.
9. Set your timer for thirty minutes and let them know that they are to complete the assignment independently.
10. Before beginning work, call the names of the students whose cards you set aside and meet with them for help.
11. Send these students back to work independently when they've shown you they now understand the concept.

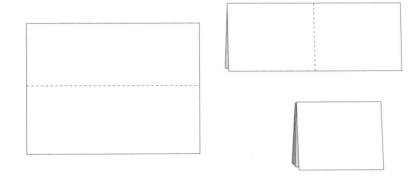

FIG. 3-5

"Fold it once. Fold it twice. Keep it folded."

Tournament Seeding

One of our many classroom "toys" is a tournament ladder. Using a broad-tipped felt pen and a ruler, I drew one on a piece of tag board. I then had it laminated so that we could write on it with a dry erase pen—the kind of pen used on white boards.

Now, whenever we feel like having a tournament (spell-offs, multiplication flash card competitions, etc.), we use the cards to randomly "seed the tournament."

First, I'll shuffle the deck and hand it to a student assistant. My assistant will then read the names one at a time as I fill in the slots. In a matter of minutes our tournament is set, and we're ready for the start of the first round.

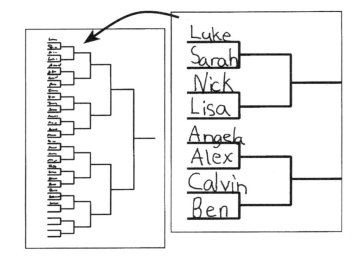

FIG. 3-6
This laminated tournament chart makes it easy to organize classroom competitions.

Extra Decks

Don't feel you have to limit yourself to just one set of cards. Make as many sets as you wish to fill as many needs as you can.

For example, you could make a special deck of cards for calling upon students to read orally. Although you could use your regular set of Class Cards for this purpose, research seems to indicate that it's not always in a child's best interests to be forced to read aloud in front of his peers. (This is especially true if you're reading from English language textbooks and English is not the primary language of some of your students.) Why not make a volunteer deck?

Announce to your class that you need students to read aloud. Take down names of students who volunteer and make a set of cards with just those names. Use this deck whenever you need students to read aloud.

> I realize that not everyone will be reading. However, you will be creating a secure and protective environment in which no one is allowed to laugh or tease the volunteer readers about their reading skills. This helps to promote a sense of safety: another one of the five basic student needs. This base of security fosters a willingness to participate in oral reading. Speaking from experience, I've found that more and more of my students ask to have their names added to the volunteer deck after they've experienced the fact that the volunteer readers are treated with respect and dignity.

Suggestion: You might not want to use the same type of cards as you used for your "main deck." With smaller groups of students, plain 3 X 5 index cards will work just great. Or, for an easier-to-handle "mini" deck, cut 4 X 6 index cards in half.

Extra Cards

Before I share some ideas for adding cards to your basic set, please exercise a bit of caution. The "extra card" ideas are for later on after you and the students have had a chance to get used to your Class Cards. At first, just keep everything nice and simple.

Add your own card to the deck.
Use one of the leftover cards from your kit and write your name at both ends. When your card is drawn, say your own name and offer your response.

FIG. 3-7
Why not call upon yourself?

Caution: Make sure you have an answer prepared before drawing a card. You wouldn't want to see your own name and then grope about trying to quickly solve the three place multiplication problem you were asking them to do. (Someone once said, "Teaching by example is not just one way of teaching, it's the only way." You can't expect them to be prepared if you're not making the same effort yourself.)

Include cards for characters in novels you may be studying.

A teacher shared this trick with me. She and her students were reading "Sarah, Plain and Tall" as a class project. During the month when they were studying the book, she added extra cards to the deck. The cards added represented characters from the book. For the first week, she added a card with Anna's name on it. (Obviously, you would have a problem with this variation if one of your own students were named Anna.) During the second week, she replaced "Anna's card" with one for Caleb. For the final two weeks she used a card with Sarah's name on it.

Whenever one of these extra cards was drawn and the name was called, students would raise hands to volunteer a response. In order to be allowed to respond, though, they had to first share some thought about that particular character.

Think about all of the information that would be shared about these characters during the week as students volunteered to take their place.

"Where's Waldo?"

Another teacher modification, similar to the idea about using extra cards for the main characters in a novel, was to make a card for Waldo—the little guy with the red and white clothes who always wants us to find him. This new card was kept in the teacher's desk along with a small, plastic replica of Waldo he had purchased. Then, when the students were not present, he would place Waldo somewhere in the room so that he was visible to everyone. Once Waldo was "hidden," his card was added to the deck. When Waldo's name was called during card use, the kids would quickly scan the room for Waldo. The first one to "find Waldo" would raise a hand. When called upon, they would point to Waldo and be allowed to respond. Pretty cute idea, eh?

Have two decks of cards, one red and one blue.

By having two decks, you'll afford yourself the opportunity of calling upon the same student twice without having to reshuffle the cards. This would be a good technique for any students who erroneously think that they can relax because their cards have already been drawn. And, by having one red deck and one blue deck, you'll be able to separate them quickly whenever you need just one deck for some activity such as randomly placing students in informal work groups.

If the size of your class is twenty-six or less, you can accomplish the "two decks" idea with just one deck of cards. All you have to do is write one set of names on the red cards—hearts and diamonds—and a duplicate set of names on the black cards—clubs and spades. Then, when you want just a single deck, you could have one of your students separate the cards by suit. Hearts and diamonds would go in one pile while clubs and spades went into another pile.

If you have students sit together in cooperative learning groups, you can add a card for each team.
We have six teams of students in our room. The teams are identified by color: red, orange, yellow, green, blue, violet. In my deck of cards are six extra cards, one per team. When one of the team cards appears during card use, I'll call out the team color. That team is then allowed to conference and decide upon an appropriate response. I continue calling upon individual students.

When the team reaches its decision, a member of the team stands and waits to be called upon to share the team's answer. Team cards makes for a nice informational change of pace in that we supplement the ideas of individual students by allowing for some collaboration.

Use the jokers.

Just about every deck of playing cards comes with two jokers. You might want to include one of them in your set of Class Cards. This card would act as a "wild card" and could be used in a variety of ways.

Open response
Make up a fake name for the wild card. "Hershel" will do as an example. Whenever the joker comes up in the deck, call on Hershel as if he were a student. The response procedure in this case would be the same as when you call on someone who is absent. Students wishing to respond will raise a hand. When you pick someone, this student must first ask, "May I take Hershel's place?"

Student bonus
The wild card comes up and is shown to the class. The next card is drawn, and the student is called on to respond. A correct response earns that student some simple reward such as a sticker, a handful of sunflower seeds, a standing ovation, or what have you.

Class bonus
It's the same procedure as the Student Bonus except that correct responses earn the entire class a point. Keep track of the points in some visible way. Set

a goal: twenty points earns the class some extra recess time.

Joke telling

Middle school teacher Carole Pollard keeps a joke book handy in class. Whenever the joker appears, she'll stop and read a quick joke to the class. What a nice way to keep things light and lively.

Errands

To simplify the selection of students for special jobs—running errands, assisting the teacher, playing messenger, etc.—and avoid showing any undue favoritism, you can easily rely upon your Class Cards.

Method One
Pick a card at random whenever a student helper is needed.

Method Two
Pick a card at the beginning of the day. The student whose card you've drawn will be your helper all day long.

FIG. 3-8
A special desk marker will identify your Helper of the Day.

Record Keepers

A friend of mine was experiencing some difficulty with her fourth graders during their daily health lesson. This lesson was the last one before lunch, and she felt that their attention was lagging and needed a boost of some sort. Her solution? She came up with a simple, yet effective, variation on the basic Class Cards idea.

She first made a new set of Class Cards using unlined, green 3 X 5 index cards. (Color-coding sets of cards makes them easier to manage.) Since this deck was made with index cards, she would be able to mark on them with a pencil. By using these new Class Cards during the health lessons, she would have the ability to keep a simple record of how the students were performing.

She gave these cards a try the very next day. As they moved through the health lesson, she called on students to respond[†] using her new "Health Deck."

Positive responses received a **+** and were placed in one pile. The negative responses were marked with a **–** and placed in a separate pile.

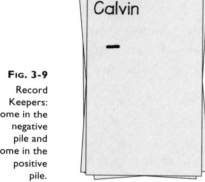

Fig. 3-9
Record Keepers: some in the negative pile and some in the positive pile.

By the end of that day's health lesson, everyone had had an opportunity to respond in some way. To dismiss them for lunch, she first picked up the **+** pile. These students were identified and sent to lunch. The remaining group of students, the ones who had received a **–** for their responses, were in need of some type of intervention. Her dialogue might have gone something like this:

> TEACHER
>> (Looking through the – cards.)
>>> *For some reason you were not staying with today's health lesson. Now, I know for a fact that the health assignment for today was on the board this morning,*
>> (pointing to page numbers on chalkboard)
>>> *and that the vocabulary words for today were listed. And I seem to re-member bringing this to everyone's attention this morning with the suggestion that you look it over if you had any free time. Now then, are we going to be learning about health tomorrow?*

[†] Remember, responses are not always specific answers to specific questions. Imagine, for example, that the class is reading orally from the textbook. If a student, when called on to read, begins promptly, a + would be recorded. Conversely, a student who is not following the lesson and does not know where to begin reading when called on would receive a – mark on his card. Response opportunities can be as varied as the teaching strategies being employed.

STUDENTS
(Lots of head nodding.)

TEACHER
Right you are. Will I be using this deck of cards
(waving green health cards in front of group)
to call upon students?

STUDENTS
(More head nodding.)

TEACHER
Right again. Please pay better attention tomorrow. Any questions? Enjoy your lunch.

Regardless of what was actually said to these students, they were made to understand that the teacher was aware of, and concerned about, their daily progress. This important realization on the part of the students can be a key motivational factor.

Bonus: Using cards you can mark on will provide you with a record of each student's effort in one particular subject. Along with the "muscle" they'll add to your daily interactions, a deck of Record Keepers will act as a handy reference guide at report card time.

Red Hands

If you've taught for more than a week, then you already know how annoying it is to be in the middle of a question-answer session with your students only to have one of them blurt out an answer. It's a real drag on you and the other students to remind someone over and over again to raise a hand before responding. Well, remind no more. With this little paper tool you'll be able to act upon your expectations of behavior and not just talk about them.

Red Hands are cut from red construction paper using an Ellison die cutter. They are kept on my desk. Whenever a student blurts out an answer or response when it is inappropriate to do so, I stop everything, pick up one of the Red Hands, and extend it to the blurter. He is then required to go over to our Counseling Center—a desk in the back of the room—where he writes his name and the date on the hand. The hand is then dropped into a plastic container that "holds hands."

FIG. 3-10
Calvin has written his name and the day's date on the red hand he was given for blurting out an answer.

At the end of the week, one of the students goes through the container and records the hands on a grade sheet. The students with the most Red Hands have them stapled to Student Bulletins *(blackline master in the appendix)* which are then sent home. It's this type of specific, goal-oriented communication that really gets results. We're not saying that Calvin is completely irresponsible. He just needs to exercise a bit more self-control.

STUDENT BULLETIN

Name _Calvin_

Date _Oct. 24_

A **Red Hand** means:
• *blurting out an answer*
• *not waiting to be called upon*

A **Green Hand** means:
• *raising a hand to speak*
• *waiting patiently for a turn*

Teacher signature _Mr. Morris_   Parent signature _____

FIG. 3-11
The "red hands" that Calvin received during the week were stapled to this special Student Bulletin and sent home.

Red Hand Recommendation: At the end of the week, you could recognize or reward everyone who did not have any hands in the container by stapling a Green Hand to the bulletin. Or, you could check the grade sheet and praise a student who had 8 hands last week but only 3 this week. Consistent acknowledgement of this sort will encourage them to abide by your classroom rules.

A Note for the Sub

Here's something you can do for the next substitute teacher who will be spending the day in your room. Letting them know we care will help them to feel more like fellow educators and less like hired help. And, since Class Cards will be making your days at school so much easier, why not share the wealth? How about leaving a brief note attached to your deck of Class Cards that explains their use? It doesn't need to be novel-length; just a couple of sentences outlining the concept. *(A sample note can be found in the appendix.)* This brief note, along with the helpful hints the students will want to add on their own, will be a great way to make the substitute teacher feel right at home.

You might even want the sub to use a set of Record Keepers *(page 46)* and do some simple documentation of student effort while you're away for the day.

All in all, Class Cards can be a handy little tool no matter who happens to be using them.

Stretching Exercises

The idea I hope I've expressed in this last chapter is one of extension. After all, the basic idea is relatively simple. It's what you do with it, what you're able to accomplish with it, that is so important.

From the very first day you put Class Cards to work in your room, and for as long as you use them, try to extend their application so that they continue to supply the students' needs in new ways. Think of additional strategies you could employ to take advantage of this refreshingly simple tool.

Keep your eyes and senses open as you use your cards. Find out what works and what doesn't. Create your own variations to fit your own needs. Involve the students whenever possible.

Please don't get the feeling, though, that you have to discover new ideas right away. It will take you a bit of time to develop your own methods. You'll have to live with Class Cards for awhile before new ideas will flow; nonetheless, once used, flow they will.

After twenty years of use, I still marvel at the simplicity, the effectiveness, and the incredible power of my Class Cards.

Appendix

Red Hand Blackline

A Note for the Sub

Catalog of Products

A Word About Class Cards

Dear Visiting Teacher,

Welcome to our room. We hope you enjoy your stay today and that the experience will be a pleasant one.

I've left you a teaching tool that should really help you as you interact with the students. It's a deck of cards with the names of the students written on them. There is one card for each student. I use them for all kinds of things:

- ✓ calling on students during lessons,
- ✓ choosing students to answer questions,
- ✓ taking turns during games,
- ✓ selecting special helpers,
- ✓ etc., etc., etc.

Basically, I just shuffle the cards and then start calling upon students as their cards appear. It's simple, effective, and fair. You might want to give the deck a try and see what you think.

Sincerely,

P.S. The students love it when I use the cards.

STUDENT BULLETIN

Name _____

Date _____

A **Red Hand** means:
- *blurting out an answer*
- *not waiting to be called upon*

A **Green Hand** means:
- *raising a hand to speak*
- *waiting patiently for a turn*

Teacher signature _____   Parent signature _____

STUDENT BULLETIN

Name _____

Date _____

A **Red Hand** means:
- *blurting out an answer*
- *not waiting to be called upon*

A **Green Hand** means:
- *raising a hand to speak*
- *waiting patiently for a turn*

Teacher signature _____   Parent signature _____

NEW MANAGEMENT PRODUCTS
BY RICK MORRIS

Books
Teaching Guides
Classroom Tools

"…in touch with today's educators."

Rick's newest invention!

Binder Stand®

Turns any 3-ring binder into an easy-to-use desktop display!

1. Insert instruction sheet in your 3-ring binder.

2. Attach Binder Stand® to both covers.

3. Place on top of desk or table.

Binder Stand®

set of 3 $8.00

US PATENT PENDING

---

http://www.newmanagement.com

Get more information about our products or **order on-line with a credit card.**

New Feature! You can now download teaching guides, blackline masters, and more. Just go to **Classroom Tips** *and click on the* **Download Files** *link.*

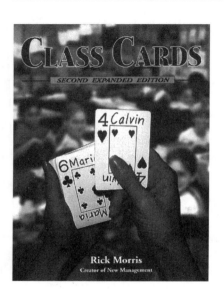

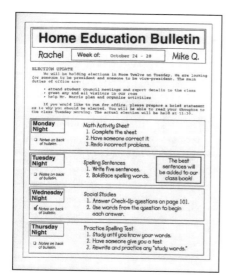

The Home Education Bulletin

*The New Management System
for building a successful home learning program*

This easy-to-follow teacher's guide will show you how to start your own homework communication tool for improving the quality and effort your students put into their home studies. A real parent favorite, The Home Education Bulletin comes complete with samples, suggestions, and a set of blackline masters.

$3.00

*Teacher's Guide • Sample Bulletin
Grade Keeping Suggestions • Blackline Masters*

Sentence Strips:
Cut and Paste Paragraphs

*The New Management technique
for successful student writing*

Sentence Strips is a new and powerful way for students to gain writing confidence and become more proficient writers. Originally published in *The Writing Notebook,* this recently revised version is a sixteen-page mini-guide which provides step-by-step instructions for incorporating this simple yet effective technique into your existing written language program.

$3.00

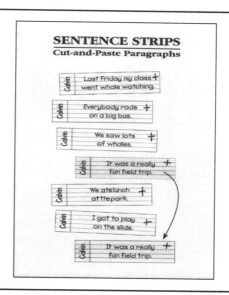

FLIP WRITER: The Fun Way to Learn Cursive!

These amazing flip books make cursive come alive. By fanning the pages of the book, your students will actually see cursive letters being created before their eyes.

Ideally suited for initial instruction, remediation, or as a handy reference guide for independent student use, this playful learning device will have your students forming letters properly in no time.

Book 1: Lowercase or Book 2: Uppercase $10.00 each   **Buy both as a set $18.00**

*We guarantee
that your class
will love these
books, or we'll
buy 'em back!*

QUICK PICK

*Lottery Toy for Randomly
Selecting Students*

Quick Pick is a hand-held plastic device that's powered by a AA battery. When you press the button in the handle, the little numbered balls inside the globe begin to whirl around. Rather quickly, some of the balls will exit through a small opening in the globe and end up in the tube next to the handle. The numbers tell me which students to call on to be the helpers.

The beauty of the design is that you can adjust the number of balls to match the number of students you have. You just remove the plug in the bottom of the tube and take out the numbers you don't need.

Bonus: The sound of the balls rolling around inside the globe makes for a nice attention getter.

My students love this playful little toy.

Quick Pick™ lottery toy
$7.00
(Packaged with one AA battery.)

LATE WORK STAMPS

*Rubber Stamps for Marking Unfinished Assignments
Available in both English and Spanish*

*The Late Work Stamp
is a high quality
rubber stamp that
will last for years.*

English or Spanish $8.00 each   **Buy both as a set $15.00**

"3 R" STAMP

*Rubber Stamp for Acknowledging Students
Who Exhibit Responsible Behavior*

*Our Room Twelve
Class Pledge:*

*"As a member of Room Twelve, I pledge to **respect** myself by making good choices, **respect** my neighbors by treating them kindly, and take **responsibility** for all of my actions."*

"3 R" Stamp $8.00

✓ **WORKS WITH KNOBS OR HANDLES**

✓ **ELIMINATES BOTHERSOME DOOR NOISE**

✓ **REDUCES CLASSROOM DISTRACTIONS**

✓ **FACILITATES ENTRY FOR PHYSICALLY CHALLENGED STUDENTS**

✓ **HANGS FROM INTERIOR KNOB WHEN NOT IN USE**

Research Identifies Door as #1 Classroom Distraction

In a recent study on classroom distractions, the sound of the door opening and closing was found to be the biggest distraction of them all. That's why Rick Morris invented DOOR BLØK.

Its simple, functional design prevents the door from closing fully. Not only is the sound of the closing door gone, but so is the rattling of the knob as students come and go. A simple push or pull on the door and it opens and closes silently.

DOOR BLØK $5.00

"I can't imagine trying to keep my class on schedule without a digital timer."

—James Sutter
Sixth Grade Teacher
Elk Grove Unified School District

Without a doubt, a digital timer is the most underutilized piece of technology available to teachers. Whether you need to monitor the length of an independent work period or merely ensure that each of your five student teams has a fair turn at every learning center, you'll soon discover as other teachers already have: a digital timer is an indispensable classroom tool.

I've tried a dozen different models and really like this new one from Sunbeam that is both a count up and count down timer. It also has: 1) a memory function; 2) a clip; and 3) a magnet on the back so that you can attach it to your white board. Two thumbs way up.

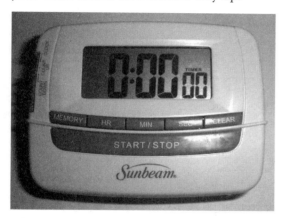

Sunbeam® Digital Timer
"Digi-Master"
$15.00
(Packaged with one AA battery.)

TIME TIMER®
Generaction Co.

Large display, silent action, easy-to-set, easy-to-read.

Invented by a mother to help her daughter get ready for preschool, the Time Timer is a wonderfully simple tool. The large clock face enables it to be seen from across the room while the red "pie shape" provides a quick sense of the time remaining. (Runs on a single AA battery; not included.)

Sold in catalogs for $30 plus tax, shipping, and handling.

Our price: $25 (tax included)

Teach time management skills on any standard overhead projector or desk top with this versatile classroom tool. *TeachTimer* functions as a timer, a clock, or a chronometer to bring time awareness to virtually any classroom activity.

New Feature!
Adjustable 0-5 minute Pre-alarm warning

TeachTimer
Stokes Publishing Company

Place this timer on your overhead projector and it will display a large, clear image that can be viewed from just about anywhere in your classroom. This new model comes with an adjustable 0-5 minute pre-alarm warning.

Bonus: TeachTimer's foldable legs allow it to function as a desk top timer for use by small groups.

Sold in catalogs for $45 plus tax, shipping, and handling.

Our price: $40 (tax included)

ORDER FORM

Books

New Management Handbook
How to Create a Happier, More Productive Classroom

Tools & Toys
Fifty Fun Ways to Love Your Class

Class Cards
How to Put Your Class in the Palm of Your Hand

Teaching Guides

The Home Education Bulletin

Sentence Strips
Cut-and-Paste Paragraphs

Classroom Tools

Flip Writers
Lowercase and Uppercase Cursive

Late Work Stamps
English and Spanish Versions

"3 R" Stamp

Quick Pick - lottery toy

DOOR BLØK™

Binder Stand®

Sunbeam Digital Timer

Time Timer - Red Dial

Teach Timer - Overhead

#	Item	Price	Cost
	New Mgmt Handbook	24.95	
	Tools & Toys book	12.95	
	Class Cards book	6.95	
	Home Education Bulletin	3.00	
	Sentence Strips	3.00	
	Flip Writers - 2 book set	18.00	
	Late Work Stamp - English	8.00	
	Late Work Stamp - Spanish	8.00	
	2 stamp set - Eng & Span	15.00	
	"3 R" Stamp	8.00	
	Quick Pick - lottery toy	7.00	
	DOOR BLØK	5.00	
	Binder Stand (set of 3)	8.00	
	Sunbeam Digital Timer	15.00	
	Time Timer - red dial	25.00	
	Teach Timer - overhead	40.00	

Shipping & Handling rates		
up to $40 ... $5.00 $41 to $60 ... $6.00 $61 to $80 ... $7.00 $81 to $100 ... $8.00	over $100 10% of Sub-Total	**Sub-Total**
		S & H
		TOTAL

(Please note: Prices shown above include sales tax.)

SHIP THIS ORDER TO:

_____
Name

_____
Address

_____
City   State   ZIP

FORM OF PAYMENT:

☐ Cash ☐ Check ☐ Money order ☐ MasterCard ☐ VISA

Credit Card Number: Expiration Date:

└─┴─┴─┴─┘ └─┴─┴─┴─┘ └─┴─┴─┴─┘ └─┴─┴─┴─┘   └─┴─┘ └─┴─┘

_____ _____
Print name as it appears on card   Cardholder signature

_____
Telephone number (for credit verification only)

MAIL PAYMENT AND ORDER FORM TO:
New Management
6512 Edmonton Avenue
San Diego, CA 92122